BUNNIES
FROM HEAD TO TAIL

By Emmett Martin

Gareth Stevens
PUBLISHING

Please visit our website, www.garethstevens.com. For a free color catalog of all our high-quality books, call toll free 1-800-542-2595 or fax 1-877-542-2596.

Library of Congress Cataloging-in-Publication Data

Names: Martin, Emmett, author.
Title: Bunnies from head to tail / Emmett Martin.
Description: New York : Gareth Stevens Publishing, [2021] | Series: Animals from head to tail | Includes index.
Identifiers: LCCN 2019042313 | ISBN 9781538255322 (library binding) | ISBN 9781538255308 (paperback) | ISBN 9781538255315 (6 pack) | ISBN 9781538255339 (ebook)
Subjects: LCSH: Rabbits–Juvenile literature.
Classification: LCC QL737.L32 M379 2021 | DDC 599.32–dc23
LC record available at https://lccn.loc.gov/2019042313

First Edition

Published in 2021 by
Gareth Stevens Publishing
111 East 14th Street, Suite 349
New York, NY 10003

Copyright © 2021 Gareth Stevens Publishing

Editor: Therese Shea
Designer: Laura Bowen

Photo credits: Cover, p. 1 Andrea Izzotti/Shutterstock.com; p. 5 Elena Masiutkina/Shutterstock.com; p. 7 (top left) Jeroen Mikkers/Shutterstock.com; p. 7 (top right) Irykdelta/Shutterstock.com; p. 7 (bottom left) goja1/Shutterstock.com; p. 7 (bottom right) Kimbomac/Shutterstock.com; p. 9 Barat Roland/Shutterstock.com; p. 11 Marchenko Denis/Shutterstock.com; p. 13 Geza Farkas/Shutterstock.com; pp. 15, 24 (burrow) AfriramPOE/Shutterstock.com; p. 17 Mary Lynn Strand/Shutterstock.com; p. 19 HGalina/Shutterstock.com; p. 21 Anupong Thiprot/Shutterstock.com; pp. 23, 24 (colony) William Booth/Shutterstock.com.

Printed in the United States of America

Some of the images in this book illustrate individuals who are models. The depictions do not imply actual situations or events.

CPSIA compliance information: Batch #CS20GS: For further information contact Gareth Stevens, New York, New York at 1-800-542-2595.

Find us on

Contents

Bunnies are rabbits!
They have soft fur.

There are 29 kinds!

Bunnies have long ears.

They have a short tail.

11

Bunnies have strong legs.
They can jump far!

13

Bunnies live in burrows.
They dig them in the dirt.

Bunnies thump their legs.
That means danger!

Bunnies eat plants.

19

Baby bunnies have no fur.
Their eyes are shut.

Bunnies live in groups.
This is a colony!

Words to Know

burrow

colony

Index

24